Things to Know About the Altman Z-score

First published by Kjøller 2023

Disclaimer:

The information contained in this book is provided for general informational purposes only. While every effort has been made to ensure that the information is accurate and up-to-date, The Author makes no representations or warranties of any kind, express or implied, about the completeness, accuracy, reliability, suitability, or availability with respect to the information, products, services, or related graphics contained in the book for any purpose.

The Author disclaims any liability for any loss or damage, including without limitation, indirect or consequential loss or damage, or any loss or damage whatsoever arising from loss of data or profits arising out of, or in connection with, the use of this book.

Readers are solely responsible for determining the appropriateness of the information contained in this book for their specific purposes and should seek professional advice before acting upon any information contained herein. The Author shall not be liable for any damages of any kind arising from the use of this book or the information contained herein.

Table of Contents

Introduction

This book is a handy tool for anyone trying to navigate the world of finance, business and accounting. It provides a collection of terms, definitions and explanations of various concepts, theories and models to help readers understand the complexities of corporate finance. One of the crucial concepts covered in this book is the Altman Z-Score, a financial model used to measure a company's financial stress and the likelihood of its bankruptcy.

In today's highly competitive business environment, it's vital for managers, investors and other stakeholders to be able to assess a company's financial position accurately. The Altman Z-Score is a widely accepted tool that allows them to do so objectively, by using a handful of financial ratios and other variables that reflect a company's financial health. This book defines the Altman Z-Score term and provides a comprehensive overview of how it works and why it's crucial in financial analysis. It also covers related concepts such as the Altman Z-Score formula, limitations, and how to interpret the results.

Acid-test ratio

Another financial ratio used in the Altman Z-score model that measures a company's ability to pay off its short-term liabilities without relying on the sale of inventory. It is calculated by dividing a company's current assets (excluding inventory) by its current liabilities. A higher acid-test ratio indicates that a company has sufficient liquid assets to cover its short-term liabilities.

Altman Z-score

A statistical model developed by Edward Altman in 1968 that is used to predict the likelihood of a company experiencing financial distress within the next two years. The score is based on five financial ratios, including working capital to total assets, retained earnings to total assets, earnings before interest and taxes to total assets, market value of equity to book value of total liabilities, and sales to total assets.

Asset turnover ratio

A financial ratio used in the Altman Z-score model that measures a company's ability to generate revenue from its assets. It is calculated by dividing a company's sales by its total assets. A high asset turnover ratio indicates that a company is efficiently using its assets to generate revenue.

Balance Sheet

The balance sheet is the financial statement that highlights an organization's assets, liabilities, and shareholder equity at a specific point in time. The balance sheet gives a snapshot of the financial status of an organization.

Bankruptcy

A state where an organization or individual is indebted to such an extent that they are unable to pay their debts. Bankruptcy can lead to liquidation of assets, may take an extended duration, and lead to negative credit scores.

Bankruptcy Prediction

Bankruptcy prediction is a statistical analysis model that predicts an organization's likelihood to declare bankruptcy. This is done by analyzing a company's financial statements and other external factors, such as macroeconomic policies and information from the industry it belongs to.

Bankruptcy Risk

Bankruptcy risk is the chance of an organization failing to meet its debt obligations and eventually filing for bankruptcy. If an organization has a high bankruptcy risk, it may result in more debt to equity ratio, reducing the organization's profitability, goodwill, and business growth.

Beta

Beta relates to a measure of a stock's volatility in relation to the market. If a company's beta is higher than the market's average rate, its stock can be considered volatile; if less than the average, the stock can be deemed stable. Beta is useful in determining a stock's risk and return.

Blue-Chip

Relates to a company or stock that is highly regarded due to its consistent growth, market dominance, stable earnings, and a long-standing reputation. Organizations that are considered blue-chip are widely known and highly stable, making their stocks less susceptible to volatility compared to other up-and-coming or smaller companies.

Bond

A financial instrument that allows an organization to borrow capital. It comprises paying periodic interest to the bondholder and repayment of the borrowed principal upon maturity of the bond. The bond issuing organization is called the issuer, and the bondholder is called the lender or investor.

Business Failure

Business failure occurs when an organization stops operating after encountering several challenges, including bankruptcy, financial distress, or severe losses. The loss of a business can impact its employees, shareholders, and creditors, leading to financial distress and long-term consequences.

Business Risk

The likelihood of failure faced by an organization due to internal or external factors. Internal factors such as bad management, employees, or systems, while external risks are those beyond the organization's control.

Capitalization

Capitalization refers to the total amount of debt and equity that a company uses to finance its operations. The amount of capitalization a company has affects its risk profile and creditworthiness. Higher capitalization increases the risk and makes creditors more wary to lend. This factor is included in the Altman Z-Score scoring system, as well.

Cash Flow

Cash flow is the amount of cash generated by a company during a specific period. It is calculated as the company's cash inflows minus its cash outflows. Altman Z-Score, which is a financial model, incorporates a company's cash flow as one of the criteria for evaluating it. If a company's cash flow is good, then it stands a higher chance of obtaining a higher score on the Z-score.

Cash Ratio

The cash ratio is a financial ratio that shows the amount of cash and cash equivalents that a company can use to pay off its current liabilities. Cash ratio is a direct measure of liquidity and positions the company can move quickly to settle its debts. This ratio is also used as an indicator of the company's short-term liquidity and financial health.

Competitive Environment

Competitive environment refers to the current state of the industry that the company is operating in. The Altman Z-score model takes this into account as it evaluates a company's financial risk profile.

Coverage Ratio

The Coverage ratio is a financial ratio that is calculated as earnings before interest and taxes (EBIT) divided by interest expense. The ratio helps creditors assess a company's ability to meet its debt obligations. It's also included in the Altman Z-Score formula.

Credit Risk

Credit risk is the risk of default on a loan or any financial obligation by the borrower. Altman Z-Score includes factors that help assess a borrower's credit risk so that the lender can decide whether to grant credit or not.

Credit Score

Credit Score is a numerical value that represents a borrower's creditworthiness. The score is generated by accounting for various factors such as payment history, outstanding balances, age of credit, types of credit accounts, etc. The Altman Z-Score model incorporates a company's credit score as part of how it evaluates the company's creditworthiness.

Current Liabilities

Current liabilities represent the debts and obligations of a company that need to be settled within one year. They usually include accounts payable, salaries and wages payable, taxes payable, and other short-term obligations. The Altman Z-Score model analyses the relationship between current assets and current liabilities to determine if the company has the ability to pay its debts on time.

Current Ratio

The current ratio is the ratio that measures a company's ability to pay its debts and obligations within one year with its current assets. The formula to calculate the current ratio is dividing the company's current assets by its current liabilities. It is used as an indicator of the company's short-term liquidity and financial health.

Debt Service Coverage Ratio

A financial ratio that measures a company's ability to pay off its debt obligations based on its cash flow. This ratio is not included in the Altman Z-score calculation, but it can be used as a complementary measure of financial health.

Debt to Asset Ratio

A financial ratio that measures the percentage of a company's assets that are financed by debt. This ratio is included in the Altman Z-score calculation as one of the predictors.

Debt to Equity Ratio

A financial ratio that measures the amount of debt a company has relative to its shareholder equity. This ratio is included in the Altman Z-score calculation as one of the predictors.

Default Risk

The risk of a borrower defaulting on their financial obligations, such as loans or bonds. The Altman Z-score is commonly used to assess default risk among corporations.

Discriminant Analysis

A statistical technique used to determine the relationship between a set of predictors and a categorical outcome variable. The Altman Z-score is derived from a discriminant analysis of financial ratios.

Distress

Refers to the financial state of a company where it is unable to pay off its debts and is at risk of bankruptcy. The Altman Z-score is used to determine the likelihood of distress and bankruptcy by calculating a score based on financial ratios.

Distress Probability

The probability that a company will experience financial distress within a given timeframe. The Altman Z-score can be used to estimate this probability.

Distress Zone

A range of Altman Z-score values where a company is considered to be at risk of financial distress or bankruptcy. This zone is typically between 1.8 and 2.7 according to Altman's original model.

Dividend Payout Ratio

The percentage of earnings that are paid out as dividends to shareholders. This ratio is not included in the Altman Z-score calculation, but it can be used as a proxy for financial stability.

Double-Declining Balance Depreciation

A method of depreciation used to accelerate the write-off of an asset's value. This method can negatively impact a company's financial ratios and increase its Z-score.

EBIT

Earnings before interest and taxes (EBIT) is a measure of a company's profitability. The Altman Z-score includes EBIT as one of several factors in determining a company's financial health. A high EBIT value indicates that a company is generating substantial profits before accounting for taxes and interest expenses.

Ebitda

Earnings before interest, taxes, depreciation, and amortization (EBITDA) is another measure of a company's profitability. The Altman Z-score takes into account a company's EBITDA value, which provides a more accurate picture of a company's profitability by accounting for depreciation and amortization expenses.

Economic recession

Economic recession refers to a significant decline in economic activity, often leading to high unemployment rates, reduced income, and reduced spending. The Altman Z-score considers economic recession as a significant threat to a company's financial health as it can result in reduced demand for goods and services, lower revenue, and reduced profitability.

Efficiency

Efficiency refers to how well a company uses its resources to generate profits. The Altman Z-score takes into account a company's operating efficiency, which measures how efficiently the company is using its resources to generate profits. A high operating efficiency score is a good indicator of a company's overall financial health.

Employee productivity

Employee productivity refers to the amount of output a company generates per worker. The Altman Z-score measures a company's financial health based on various productivity measures, including employee productivity. A high level of employee productivity indicates that a company is using its human resources efficiently to generate profits.

Equity

Equity refers to the value of a company's assets minus its liabilities. The Altman Z-score measures a company's financial health based on factors such as equity, and a high equity value is a positive sign for a company's future performance.

Equity value

Equity value refers to the value of a company's shares outstanding. The Altman Z-score considers a company's equity value as an essential factor in determining its financial health, as a high equity value provides a financial cushion and can help a company weather economic downturns or event risk.

Event risk

Event risk refers to unexpected events, such as natural disasters, pandemics, or political unrest, that could adversely affect a company's financial performance. The Altman Z-score takes into account event risk as a factor that could reduce a company's financial health, especially for companies that operate in areas prone to natural disasters or geopolitical instability.

Exchange rate risk

Exchange rate risk refers to the risk that changes in currency exchange rates could adversely affect a company's financial performance. The Altman Z-score factors in exchange rate risk as a potential threat to a company's financial health, especially for companies that operate globally.

External financing

External financing refers to funds a company raises from sources other than its internal operations, such as loans or investments. The Altman Z-score takes into account a company's reliance on external financing as a factor in determining its financial health. A high reliance on external financing can be a red flag as it may indicate that a company is struggling to generate profits from its operations.

Financial Distress

When a company is considered to be in financial distress, it means that it is unable to meet its financial obligations. This may include being at risk of bankruptcy, defaulting on loans, or being unable to pay creditors.

Financial Leverage

The use of debt to finance a company's operations. Financial leverage can increase a company's profitability but also increases the risk of financial distress, particularly during economic downturns.

Financial Ratios

Ratios that are used to assess a company's financial health and performance. These ratios use data such as revenue, profitability, and debt to provide an overview of a company's financial position.

Financial Statements

Reports that provide information about a company's financial position, including its assets, liabilities, revenue, and expenses. Financial statements are used by investors, lenders, and other stakeholders to evaluate a company's performance and financial health.

Fitch Ratings

A credit rating agency that provides independent credit opinions, research, and data to businesses and investors. Fitch ratings are used to assess the creditworthiness of an issuer or security, including the likelihood of default.

Fixed Assets

Long-term assets such as buildings, machinery, and equipment that a company owns and uses in its operations. Fixed assets are important for a company's ability to generate revenue and cash flow over the long-term.

Forecasting

The process of predicting future financial performance based on historical data and trends. This process involves analyzing financial statements and other relevant data to make strategic decisions about a company's future.

Fraud Risk

The risk that a company may engage in fraudulent activities such as embezzlement, falsifying financial statements, or misappropriating funds. The Altman Z-score can provide insights into the potential for fraudulent activities within a company.

Free Cash Flow

The amount of cash generated by a company that is available for distribution to investors or used to repay debt. Free cash flow is an important measure of a company's financial health and its ability to generate cash over the long-term.

Funding Liquidity

The ability of a company to obtain funding to meet its financial obligations. Funding liquidity is important for companies to maintain a healthy financial position and avoid financial distress.

General and Administrative Expenses

General and Administrative expenses (G&A) represent the costs associated with a company's day-to-day operations, such as salaries, rent, utilities, and other overhead expenses. In the context of the Altman Z-score, G&A expenses are used to calculate the company's earnings before interest and taxes (EBIT).

General Debt Coverage Ratio

The General Debt Coverage Ratio is a financial metric that measures a company's ability to cover its debts using its cash flows. It is included in the Altman Z-score formula as an important factor that affects a company's financial risk. The higher the General Debt Coverage Ratio, the more financially stable the company is considered to be.

General Risk Margin

General Risk Margin is a factor used in the Altman Z-score formula to assess a company's overall level of financial risk. It takes into account factors such as industry trends, macroeconomic conditions, and other external risks that could affect a company's financial health.

Going Concern

Going concern refers to the long-term viability of a company. When a company is considered a going concern, it is assumed that it will continue to operate for the foreseeable future without facing any significant financial difficulties. The Altman Z-score formula takes into account a company's going concern status when assessing its risk level.

Goodwill

Goodwill refers to the excess of the purchase price paid for a company over its net tangible assets. It is an intangible asset that represents the value of a company's reputation, customer relationships, brands, and other non-physical assets. Goodwill is included in the Altman Z-score formula as an important factor that affects a company's financial risk.

Gross Margin Ratio

The Gross Margin Ratio is a financial metric that measures a company's profitability based on the difference between its revenue and cost of goods sold. This ratio is used in the Altman Z-score formula to assess a company's financial health. A high Gross Margin Ratio indicates that a company is generating a high level of profit from its sales, which is an indicator of financial stability.

Gross Operating Income

Gross Operating Income (GOI) represents a company's revenue minus its operating expenses. It is an important factor used in the Altman Z-score formula to assess a company's profitability and financial health. A high GOI indicates that a company is generating a high level of profit from its core operations.

Gross Profit

Gross Profit is a financial metric that represents a company's revenue minus its cost of goods sold. It is used in the Altman Z-score formula as an important measure of a company's financial health and profitability. A high gross profit margin indicates that a company is generating a high level of profit from its sales.

Gross Profit Margin

Gross Profit Margin represents a company's gross profit divided by its revenue. It is an important financial metric used in the Altman Z-score formula to measure a company's profitability and financial health. A high gross profit margin indicates that a company is generating a high level of profit relative to its revenue.

Gross Working Capital

Gross Working Capital is a financial metric that represents a company's current assets minus its current liabilities. It measures a company's liquidity and ability to pay off its short-term debts. The Altman Z-score includes this metric as an important factor in assessing a company's risk.

High-risk companies

These are companies that are deemed to be at high risk of bankruptcy. The Altman Z-score is used to identify these companies based on various financial ratios and indicators.

Historical financial data

These are financial data that represent the past performance of a company over a period of time. The Altman Z-score uses historical financial data to predict a company's future bankruptcy risk.

Horizontal analysis

This is a financial analysis technique that compares a company's financial performance over time. The Altman Z-score uses horizontal analysis to analyze a company's financial data from multiple periods.

Income Statements

Income statements provide financial information such as a company's revenue, operating expenses, gains, or losses. These statements can be used in calculating financial ratios such as the Altman Z-score. A positive trend in a company's operating income, revenue, or net income could indicate improved financial performance and lead to a higher Z-score.

Incomplete Financial Statements

Incomplete financial statements may not provide adequate data for calculating the Altman Z-score accurately. If a company's financial statements do not provide sufficient data on debts, assets, liabilities, or operating expenses, it may lead to an unreliable estimate of insolvency risk.

Industrial Diversification

Diversification is a term used to describe a company that operates in multiple industries, which can influence the calculation of the Altman Z-score. Companies that have a wide range of products and services can mitigate financial risk and could potentially have a higher Z-score.

Industry

The industry or sector a company operates in is another factor to consider when applying the Altman Z-score. Some industries may be more susceptible to financial distress, while others may be more stable. For example, the aviation industry faced financial challenges during the COVID-19 pandemic, which would have affected the Altman Z-score of aviation companies.

Inflation

Inflation refers to the general rise in the price level of goods and services in an economy over a specific period. Inflation affects businesses, individuals, and governments in different ways, such as reducing the purchasing power of money and impacting interest rates. Inflation can also impact a company's financial performance, particularly in terms of inventory and accounts receivable, thus affecting the Altman Z-score.

Insolvency

Insolvency is a financial state when a company cannot meet its financial obligations as they become due, which could lead to the company filing for bankruptcy. It occurs when the company's liabilities exceed its assets, or its cash flow from operations is less than its debt obligations. The Altman Z-score is a popular formula used to predict insolvency in companies.

Interest Coverage Ratio

The Interest Coverage Ratio is a financial metric that measures a company's ability to pay off its interest expenses with its earnings before interest and taxes (EBIT). A higher interest coverage ratio indicates that the company is capable of repaying its debts on time, whereas a low ratio implies that the company may have trouble paying its debts in the future. The ratio can be calculated by dividing EBIT by the total interest expenses incurred by the company.

Interest Rates

Interest rates impact a company's financial performance and can also affect the Altman Z-score. High-interest rates can lead to higher borrowing costs for companies, leading to a high debt burden and impacting the Z-score. In contrast, low-interest rates can reduce borrowing costs and may enable companies to pay off their debts more quickly, leading to a higher Altman Z-score.

Inventory Turnover Ratio

The Inventory Turnover Ratio is a financial ratio that measures how many times a company's inventory is sold and replaced during a specific period. A high inventory turnover ratio indicates that a company is efficiently selling its inventory, whereas a low ratio could imply that inventory is not selling as quickly as it should. It can be calculated by dividing the cost of goods sold by the average inventory during a specific period.

J-curve

A curved line that represents the short-term decline in financial performance (and increase in debt) expected when a company invests in a new project or enters a new market. The J-curve effect is factored into the Altman Z-score through the use of earnings before interest and taxes (EBIT).

Joint Product

A type of product produced during a common production process that cannot be separated without incurring significant costs. Joint products are important for the Altman Z-score, as they affect the valuation of inventories, which is a component in the formula for calculating the score.

Journal

A log of financial transactions and events, recorded in chronological order. The journal is used to create the financial statements used in the Altman Z-score calculation.

Journal Entry

A transaction recorded in the journal. Journal entries are the building blocks of financial statements and are critical to the Altman Z-score calculation.

J-Score

A modification of the Altman Z-score that includes an adjustment for inflation. This modification is commonly used in emerging markets or economies with high inflation rates, where financial data may not accurately reflect actual conditions.

Judgemental Adjustments

Subjective modifications made to financial statements to improve their accuracy, such as restating depreciation or inventory valuations. Judgemental adjustments have implications for the Altman Z-score, as they alter the values for important variables such as working capital and total assets.

Judgment

The process of evaluating and making informed decisions based on available data and analysis. The Altman Z-score requires judgment on the part of the analyst, as there is no hard and fast rule that determines whether a company is financially distressed or not.

Junior Debt

A type of debt that has a lower priority for payment than senior debt in the event of bankruptcy or liquidation. Junior debt is incorporated into the calculation of the Altman Z-score to gain insight into the company's riskiness.

Junk Bond

A type of speculative bond that has a high yield (and correspondingly high risk) due to its low credit rating. Junk bonds can affect the Altman Z-score calculation by increasing a company's debt-to-equity ratio.

Just-in-time (JIT)

An inventory management system in which materials and goods are only received and produced when they are needed, reducing storage costs and increasing efficiency. JIT has implications for the Altman Z-score because it affects inventory turnover and accounts payable turnover, which are used in the formula.

Kendall rank correlation coefficient

A non-parametric statistical test used to measure the strength of association between two sets of data. It is used in finance to evaluate the accuracy of financial models.

Key financial ratios

These are the most important financial ratios used to assess a company's financial health. They include profitability ratios, liquidity ratios, leverage ratios, and efficiency ratios.

Key performance indicators (KPIs)

Metrics that are used to evaluate the success of a business. In finance, KPIs can be used to assess a company's financial health and overall performance.

K-means clustering

A method of cluster analysis designed to partition a set of data into clusters based on similarity. It is commonly used in finance to identify patterns in financial data.

Knowledge discovery in databases (KDD)

A process that involves the discovery of patterns in large datasets. In finance, it is used to identify indicators that can be used in financial analyses.

Knowledge-based systems

Computer systems that are designed to analyze large amounts of data and provide decision-making support. They are used in finance to evaluate a company's financial health.

Kolmogorov-Smirnov test

A statistical test used to determine whether a sample comes from a specific distribution. It is commonly used in finance to evaluate the accuracy of financial models.

Kruskal-Wallis test

A non-parametric statistical test used to determine if there are significant differences between more than two independent groups. It is commonly used in financial analyses alongside the Altman Z-score to provide a complete evaluation of a company's financial health.

K-S test

A statistical test used to determine whether the distribution of a dataset is significantly different from a known distribution. In finance, this test is used to evaluate the accuracy of financial models.

Kurtosis

A statistical measure that quantifies the shape of a probability distribution. It is used in finance to evaluate the quality of a financial model.

Legal claim

A lawsuit or legal action taken against a company for any reason. Altman Z-score considers legal claims as part of its total liabilities metric when analyzing a company's financial health.

Lending institution

A financial institution that provides loans to individuals or businesses. Altman Z-score can be used by lending institutions to evaluate the creditworthiness of a borrower before providing a loan.

Leverage ratio

A financial metric used to determine a company's ability to meet its long-term financial obligations. The ratio is obtained by dividing the company's total debt by its equity. A higher leverage ratio indicates that a company is more reliant on debt financing. Altman Z-score uses leverage ratio as one of its five metrics to analyze a company's financial health.

Liability

A financial obligation that a company owes to another entity as a result of a past transaction. Liabilities can be current or long-term depending on when they are due. Altman Z-score considers liabilities as part of its liquidity ratio metric when analyzing a company's financial health.

Limited liability

A legal structure that provides owners of a company with limited liability for the company's debts and obligations. Altman Z-score assumes limited liability when analyzing a company's financial health, indicating that the score does not take into account the personal liability of company owners.

Liquidity ratio

A financial metric used to determine a company's ability to meet its short-term financial obligations. The ratio is obtained by dividing current assets by current liabilities. A higher liquidity ratio indicates that a company is more capable of paying off its debts on time. Altman Z-score uses liquidity ratio as one of its five metrics to analyze a company's financial health.

Liquidity risk

The possibility of a company not being able to pay off its short-term financial obligations. Altman Z-score considers liquidity ratio as one of its five metrics to analyze a company's financial health, indicating the importance of managing liquidity risk.

Long-term debt

Any financial obligation that is due more than a year from the current date. This includes bonds, loans, and other debt instruments. Altman Z-score includes long-term debt in its leverage ratio metric when analyzing a company's financial health.

Loss ratio

A financial metric used to determine the percentage of money an insurer loses compared to the amount of money it takes in. A high loss ratio indicates that the insurer is losing more money for each dollar of premium received. Altman Z-score uses loss ratio as one of its three metrics to analyze insurance company's financial health.

Low score

A score below 1.8 on the Altman Z-score scale indicates that a company is highly likely to declare bankruptcy. This score is calculated using five financial metrics

Management Efficiency Ratio

A financial ratio that measures a company's ability to generate sales using its assets and liabilities. This ratio can be used as one of the inputs in an Altman Z-score calculation to assess a company's financial health.

Margin of Safety

The difference between the intrinsic value of an investment and its current market price. A high margin of safety indicates that an investment is undervalued and has potential for future growth. The Altman Z-score can be used to assess a company's margin of safety by calculating the probability of default or financial distress.

Market Capitalization

The total value of a company's outstanding shares of stock, calculated by multiplying the current stock price by the number of shares outstanding. The market capitalization is used as an input in the Altman Z-score calculation to reflect the size of a company and its ability to meet its financial obligations.

Market Risk Premium

The additional rate of return that investors require for investing in equities rather than risk-free assets such as government bonds. The market risk premium is used as an input in the Altman Z-score calculation to reflect the level of risk associated with investing in a particular company.

Market Value of Equity (MVE)

The total value of a company's outstanding common stock, calculated by multiplying the current stock price by the number of shares outstanding. The MVE is one of the key inputs in the Altman Z-score calculation.

Mean Return

The average rate of return earned by an investment over a certain period of time. The mean return is a key input in the Altman Z-score calculation as it reflects the profitability of a company over a specific period of time.

Modified Altman Z-score

An updated version of the Altman Z-score that incorporates additional financial ratios and uses a different set of coefficients and weights to generate a numerical score. The modified Altman Z-score is designed to provide a more accurate assessment of a company's financial health and ability to meet its financial obligations.

Moody's Default Risk Service

A credit rating service that provides analysis and ratings for both private and public companies based on their credit risk. The Altman Z-score is often benchmarked against the ratings provided by Moody's to assess its accuracy and reliability.

Moody's KMV Model

A credit risk assessment model that uses market data to estimate the probability of default or credit risk of a company. This model is often used in conjunction with the Altman Z-score to provide a more comprehensive assessment of a company's financial health.

Multiple Discriminant Analysis (MDA)

A statistical technique that uses accounting data to create a predictive model for a company's financial distress. The Altman Z-score is a type of MDA model that applies weights and coefficients to multiple accounting ratios to generate a numerical score.

Negative Equity

Negative Equity occurs when a company's liabilities exceed its assets, resulting in a negative net worth. Negative Equity is a red flag for investors and indicates a company's inability to pay its debts, increasing the likelihood of bankruptcy. In the Altman Z-score, Negative Equity is an element in the formula that negatively affects a company's score.

Net Income

Net Income is a measure of a company's profitability and represents the amount of revenue that remains after all expenses have been deducted. When calculating the Altman Z-score, Net Income is one of the financial metrics considered along with Liquidity, Solvency, and Efficiency ratios.

Net Sales

Net Sales is revenue generated by a company after returns, allowances, and discounts have been subtracted. Net Sales is used in the Altman Z-score formula along with other financial ratios to determine a company's financial stability and potential for bankruptcy.

Non-Current Liabilities

Non-Current Liabilities are long-term obligations that a company is expected to pay over a period longer than one year. Examples of Non-Current Liabilities include long-term debt and pension obligations. In the Altman Z-score, Non-Current Liabilities are a component of the formula used to assess a company's level of financial risk.

Non-Manufacturing Sector

The Non-Manufacturing Sector is a term used to define the sector of the economy that is involved in providing services instead of producing tangible goods or products. In relation to the Altman Z-score, the Non-Manufacturing Sector includes industries such as finance, healthcare, and retail, which are analyzed differently from manufacturing companies due to their unique characteristics and financial ratios.

Non-Operating Items

Non-Operating Items are items on a company's financial statement that are not related to its core operations, such as gains or losses from the sale of assets or investments. When calculating the Altman Z-score, Non-Operating Items are excluded from the formula to better reflect a company's financial health based on its core operating activities.

Non-Recurring Items

Non-Recurring Items are unique and unusual transactions that occur outside of a company's typical operations, such as a one-time legal settlement. These items are usually excluded from a company's financial statements as they do not reflect the company's ongoing financial performance. In the Altman Z-score, all Non-Recurring Items are removed from the formula to provide a more accurate reflection of a company's financial situation.

Normalized EBIT

Normalized EBIT is a measure of a company's earnings before interest and taxes that adjusts for the effects of non-recurring items and adjusts for accounting policies used by the company. Normalized EBIT is used in the Altman Z-score formula in place of traditional EBIT to provide a more accurate reflection of a company's ongoing earnings.

Normalized Working Capital

Normalized Working Capital is a calculation used to provide a more accurate representation of a company's working capital by adjusting this financial ratio for seasonal or cyclical changes in a company's operations. Normalized Working Capital is included in the Altman Z-score formula to accurately reflect a company's ability to meet its short-term financial obligations.

Obligation Parameters

Obligation parameters refer to the legal and contractual obligations a company has to its stakeholders. This includes obligations to pay back loans, interest on loans, or dividends to shareholders. These obligations can have a significant impact on a company's financial health and are used to calculate the Altman Z-Score, which looks at how well a company can meet these obligations.

Observation Period

The observation period is the timeframe used by the Altman Z-score model to analyze a company's financial performance. Generally, the observation period spans over the last fiscal year. The model uses financial ratios based on the observation period to calculate the Altman Z-Score, which is a predictor of a company's probability of bankruptcy.

Open Market

Open market refers to a free and competitive marketplace where buyers and sellers come together for trade in a specific product or service. It is a market where the price of the goods or services is controlled by supply and demand. The Altman Z-score can be used by investors to evaluate companies that trade on the open market and make informed decisions about whether to invest.

Operating Cash Flow

Operating cash flow is a financial metric used to measure the cash generated from a company's core business operations. It is calculated by subtracting operating expenses and taxes from operating income. In the Altman Z-Score model, operating cash flow is one of the metrics used to determine a company's financial strength and its ability to stay solvent.

Operating Earnings Before Depreciation

Operating Earnings Before Depreciation, commonly referred to as OEBD, is an accounting measure used by the Altman Z-Score model. It is calculated by subtracting operating expenses and depreciation from the company's revenue. This metric helps to determine the company's ability to generate profits and pay off debts.

Operating Expenses

Operating expenses refer to the expenses incurred by a company in performing its day-to-day business activities. Examples of operating expenses include rent, payroll, and utility bills. In the Altman Z-Score model, operating expenses are used to calculate the company's operating income, which helps determine its financial strength.

Operating Income

Operating income refers to the revenue generated by a company's core business operations. It is calculated by deducting the cost of goods sold, operating expenses, and depreciation from the company's revenue. Operating income is a key component in the Altman Z-Score as it provides an indication of a company's profitability and ability to generate cash flow from core operations.

Operating Profitability

Operating profitability is a financial metric used to measure the profitability of a company's core business operations. At its most basic level, this metric is calculated by dividing operating income by revenue. In the Altman Z-score, operating profitability is used to assess a company's financial standing and determine its probability of bankruptcy.

Outstanding Debt

Outstanding debt terminology refers to the amount of debt that a company has yet to pay off. Outstanding debt is a critical part of the Altman Z-Score model as it helps determine a company's leverage ratio. When a company has excessive outstanding debt, it can pose a significant risk to investors, affecting the company's long-term financial prospects.

Overhead Expenses

Overhead expenses refer to costs that are indirectly related to a company's primary business operations. Expenses such as rent, utilities, and insurance premiums are considered overhead. These costs are typically fixed and do not change, regardless of the company's sales volume. In the Altman Z-score model, the ratio of overhead expenses to revenue is used to determine a company's financial stability.

Pension obligations

Pension obligations refer to the debt that a company owes to its employees for their pension and retirement. Altman Z-score takes pension obligations into account to determine the overall financial health of a company.

Physical assets

Physical assets refer to tangible assets that a company owns, such as property or equipment. Altman Z-score takes physical assets into account to determine a company's overall financial health.

Preference shareholders

Preference shareholders are those investors in a company that have priority over common shareholders in the event of a dividend payout, bankruptcy or liquidation. Altman Z-score includes preference shareholders in calculating the overall financial health of a company.

Pre-tax earnings

Pre-tax earnings refer to a company's earnings before accounting for taxes. It is used as a key input in calculating a company's Altman Z-score.

Price-to-earnings ratio (P/E)

The price-to-earnings ratio is a valuation ratio that shows how much investors are willing to pay per dollar of earnings generated by a company. It is used to compare the relative value of different companies within the same industry.

Price-to-sales ratio (P/S)

The price-to-sales ratio is a valuation ratio that compares a company's stock price to its revenue. It is used to compare the relative value of different companies within the same industry.

Probability of default (PD)

Probability of default refers to the likelihood of a company defaulting on its debt obligations within a given period. Altman Z-score uses PD as a key input to determine the overall financial health of a company.

Productivity

Productivity measures the efficiency of a company in regards to its production processes. Increases in productivity can lead to higher profits, which can contribute to a company's overall financial health.

Profitability

Profitability measures a company's ability to generate profits from its operations. A higher profitability ratio indicates that the company is effectively managing its costs, expenses and generating sales/revenue.

Purchasing power

Purchasing power refers to the value of money in terms of its ability to purchase goods and services. It can influence the overall financial health of a company by impacting consumer spending and interest rates.

Ratio Analysis

A method that compares different financial ratios to determine a company's performance and financial health. Altman Z-score includes several ratios such as working capital, retained earnings, earnings before interest and tax, sales, and total assets.

Receivables Age

The average number of days it takes a company to collect payments from its customers. The Altman Z-score uses this metric to assess a company's liquidity and ability to generate cash flow.

Receivables Turnover Ratio

A ratio that measures the number of times a company collects its average accounts receivable balance in a year. The Altman Z-score considers this ratio as a measure of a company's liquidity and ability to collect cash from its customers.

Recession

A period of economic decline characterized by reduced consumer spending, declining GDP, high unemployment, and reduced business activity. The Altman Z-score may adjust a company's financial ratios to account for the impact of a recession on its financial performance and health.

Research and Development (R&D)

A process of creating new products, services or technologies that provide a competitive advantage to a company. The Altman Z-score may consider a company's R&D expenditure as a measure of its future earnings potential.

Restructuring

A process of changing the operational or financial structure of a company to improve its performance and profitability. The Altman Z-score may adjust a company's financial ratios to account for the impact of restructuring activities on its financial health.

Retained Earnings

A portion of a company's profits that are not distributed to shareholders as dividends but kept for reinvestment into the business. The Altman Z-score includes this metric as an indicator of a company's financial strength and ability to withstand financial shocks.

Return on Assets (ROA)

A ratio that measures a company's profitability by dividing its net income by the total assets. The Altman Z-score considers ROA as an indicator of a company's earnings potential and efficiency in using its assets.

Revenue

The income generated by a company's primary business operations before deducting expenses. The Altman Z-score considers revenue as one of the financial metrics that reflects a company's earnings potential and overall financial health.

Risk

The probability of loss or harm to a company's financial position and reputation. The Altman Z-score quantifies a company's risk using a combination of financial metrics such as liquidity, profitability, and solvency.

Score

A numerical value assigned to a company based on its financial statements and market data, used to assess its creditworthiness and risk of bankruptcy.

Securities and Exchange Commission (SEC)

A US government agency responsible for regulating and overseeing the securities industry, including the disclosure of financial information by publicly traded companies.

Shareholders

Owners of a company's stock or other securities, entitled to a portion of its profits and responsible for its performance through their voting rights at shareholder meetings.

Solvency

The ability of a company to meet its long-term financial obligations and repay its debts.

Speculation

The act of betting on future events or trends, often involving risk-taking or uncertainty.

Stability

The degree to which a company's financial situation is consistent over time, measured by analyzing its financial ratios.

Standard deviation

A measure of the variability or dispersion of a set of data points, used to assess the risk or volatility of a company's financial situation.

Statistical analysis

The process of analyzing data and drawing conclusions from it using mathematical models, used to inform decision making and assess risk.

Stock market

A public market for the trading of company stocks and other securities, used to assess the value and performance of a company and its competitors.

Substantiated

Supported by evidence or proven through data analysis, used to validate the accuracy of financial statements or other company information.

Tangible Assets

A company's physical assets such as buildings, land, machinery, and equipment. Tangible assets are used in the Altman Z-score calculation as a measure of a company's financial performance.

Tax Liability

The amount of money a company owes to the government in taxes. Tax liability is included in the Altman Z-score calculation and can have an impact on a company's financial standing.

Times Interest Earned

A financial ratio used to assess a company's ability to meet its debt obligations. Times interest earned is calculated by dividing a company's earnings before interest and taxes by its interest expense. It is one of the inputs in the Altman Z-score calculation.

Total Assets

The sum of a company's short-term and long-term assets, including cash, accounts receivable, inventory, and property. Total assets are one of the five inputs used in calculating the Altman Z-score and are an indicator of a company's ability to generate revenue.

Total Current Assets

The sum of a company's short-term assets such as cash, accounts receivable, and inventory. This is another input in the Altman Z-score and an indicator of a company's liquidity and financial health.

Total Current Liabilities

The sum of a company's current liabilities such as accounts payable, short-term loans, and taxes payable. This is another input in the Altman Z-score and measures a company's short-term financial obligations.

Trade Creditors

A type of short-term liability, trade creditors refer to a company's outstanding debts to suppliers for goods and services received on credit. Trade creditors are used as one of the inputs in the Altman Z-score calculation.

Trade Debtors

A company's outstanding debts owed to it by customers for goods and services provided on credit. Trade debtors are a measure of a company's accounts receivable and are used as an input in the Altman Z-score calculation.

Trend

A term describing the direction of a company's financial performance over time. Analyzing the trend of a company's financial data is a crucial aspect of using the Altman Z-score as it can reveal potential financial distress.

Turnover

The amount of liquidity or cash flow a company generates against its total assets over a period of time. Calculating turnover with other financial indicators is a useful way of assessing a company's financial health before using the Altman Z-score.

Uncertain future prospects

If a company's future looks uncertain, it can be at higher risk of financial distress. The Altman Z-score considers a variety of factors, including management quality, earnings potential, and competitive landscape to determine the company's future prospects.

Uncertainties in legal proceedings

Any legal proceedings against a company can have a material impact on its financial health. The Altman Z-score looks at the potential liabilities from any legal proceedings and considers them along with other factors to determine the probability of bankruptcy or financial distress.

Underfunded pension obligations

Pension obligations can become a burden on a company's financial health if they are underfunded. The Altman Z-score model includes the ratio of the company's pension and employee benefit obligations to its total assets. If this ratio is high, it can signal financial distress.

Uneven revenue streams

Having a consistent revenue stream is important to maintain financial stability. The Altman Z-score takes into account the variability of a company's revenues over the past five years to gauge how stable they are.

Unfavorable market conditions

External market conditions can have a significant impact on a company's financial health. The Altman Z-score considers the macroeconomic environment, including interest rates and GDP growth, to determine the probability of bankruptcy or financial distress.

Unnecessary expenses

Companies with high expenses relative to their revenues can be at risk of financial distress. The Altman Z-score considers the efficiency of the company's operations, including its ability to keep costs under control.

Unproductive assets

Assets that are not generating income or are underutilized can be a burden on a company's financial health. The Altman Z-score looks at the ratio of sales to fixed assets to determine whether the company's assets are productive or not.

Unreliable financial reporting

Accurate financial reporting is critical for any company. The Altman Z-score model looks at the quality and consistency of a company's financial reporting to determine the probability of bankruptcy or financial distress.

Unsecured creditors

These are creditors who do not have any collateral to secure their loans. They are at higher risk of not receiving payment in case of bankruptcy or insolvency. The Altman Z-score model considers the interest coverage ratio, which takes into account the amount of interest paid to unsecured creditors. The higher the interest coverage ratio, the more likely it is that a company will be able to pay its unsecured creditors.

Unusual gains or losses

Any unusual gains or losses can have an impact on a company's financial health. The Altman Z-score takes into account any unusual gains or losses in the last year to gauge how they might impact the company's future financial health.

Valuation

Valuation refers to the process of determining the worth of a company. Altman Z-score is often used in combination with other valuation metrics to evaluate a company's financial health. Investors use this to assess a company before making any investment decisions.

Variability

Variability refers to the degree of variation in a company's financial information over a period of time. Altman Z-score takes into consideration this variability in predicting a company's financial distress. A company with a high degree of variability is likely to have a low Altman Z-score, suggesting a higher risk of bankruptcy.

Variable Costs

Variable costs are expenses that change with the level of production or sales, such as raw materials, labor costs, and inventory. Altman Z-score uses variable costs as a financial ratio to determine a company's operational efficiency and profitability.

Vendor

A vendor is a supplier of goods or services to a company. Altman Z-score can be used to evaluate the financial stability of a vendor before engaging in a business relationship, reducing the risk of supply chain disruption.

Venture Capital

Venture capital is a form of investment in which investors provide funds to startups and early-stage companies with high potential for growth. Venture capital firms use Altman Z-score to evaluate the financial stability of companies before investing in them.

Vertical Analysis

Vertical analysis is a method of analyzing financial statements by expressing each line item as a percentage of a base figure. Altman Z-score uses this method to compare a company's financial ratios over time, identifying potential financial distress.

Viability

Viability refers to a company's ability to sustain its operations over the long term. Altman Z-score can help assess a company's viability by analyzing its financial health and predicting the likelihood of bankruptcy.

Vital Signs

Vital signs are financial ratios used to evaluate a company's financial health, such as liquidity, profitability, and solvency. Altman Z-score includes several vital signs in its formula, providing a comprehensive analysis of a company's financial health.

Volatility

Volatility refers to the degree of unpredictability in a company's financial performance. Companies with high volatility have unpredictable cash flows, which can lead to higher risk of financial distress. Altman z-score takes into account volatility and its effect on a company's financial health.

Voluntary Liquidation

Voluntary liquidation occurs when a company decides to wind down its operations voluntarily. Altman Z-score can assist in identifying the likelihood of voluntary liquidation by analyzing the company's financial health and predicting the likelihood of bankruptcy.

Weighted Scoring

A method used in the Altman Z-score formula to assign different weights to each financial variable based on its level of importance in determining a company's bankruptcy risk. For example, profitability is given a higher weight than liquidity, as profitability is considered a stronger indicator of long-term financial health.

Weighting Coefficients

The specific weights assigned to each financial variable in the Altman Z-score formula. These coefficients are determined by statistical analysis and are used to calculate a company's final bankruptcy risk score.

Willingness to Pay Ratio

A financial ratio that measures a company's ability to meet its debt obligations. The Altman Z-score formula includes this ratio as a measure of profitability, as companies with strong profitability are more likely to be able to meet their debt obligations.

Window Dressing

A practice used by some companies to manipulate their financial statements to create a more favorable image of their financial health. The Altman Z-score formula is designed to identify instances of window dressing and produce an accurate assessment of a company's bankruptcy risk.

Wireline

A telecommunications industry term that refers to fixed-line telephone services. The Altman Z-score formula includes wireline among the industries it can be applied to, along with other industries such as manufacturing, transportation, and retail.

Working Capital

The difference between a company's current assets and current liabilities. The Altman Z-score formula includes working capital as one of the five variables used to determine a company's financial health. This is because working capital measures a company's short-term liquidity, which is an important indicator of financial stability.

Working Capital to Total Assets Ratio

A financial ratio that measures the percentage of a company's total assets that are financed through working capital. This ratio is used in the Altman Z-score formula to evaluate a company's liquidity and financial stability.

Working Capital Turnover Ratio

A financial ratio that evaluates a company's ability to generate sales from its working capital. This ratio is used in the Altman Z-score formula to assess a company's efficiency in using its working capital to generate revenue.

Worst Case Scenario

The most negative outcome that could realistically occur in a given situation. The Altman Z-score formula is designed to provide a worst-case scenario assessment of a company's bankruptcy risk, giving investors and creditors a clear picture of the company's financial health even in the event of significant downturns or unforeseen events.

Years

The number of years in which a company has been in operation is an important aspect of the Altman Z-score analysis. It is used as a measure of stability and the longer a company has been in business, the more reliable it is expected to be.

Yellow Flag

A yellow flag is a warning sign indicating that a company is in financial trouble. The Altman Z-score analysis classifies a company as having a yellow flag if its Z-score is between 1.81 and 2.99, indicating that bankruptcy risk is moderate to high.

Yellow Zone

The yellow zone is the range of Z-scores between 1.10 and 2.99, indicating a moderate to high risk of bankruptcy. Companies in the yellow zone are considered to be financially distressed and may require further analysis.

Yes/No Factors

The Altman Z-score model uses a combination of qualitative and quantitative factors to assess the financial health of a company. These factors are assigned yes/no values and are used to calculate the Z-score. Some of these factors include profitability, leverage, liquidity, and solvency.

Yesterday's Information

The Altman Z-score analysis is based on financial data from previous years, which may not accurately reflect the current financial situation of a company. As such, the Z-score is just one tool in a broader analysis of a company's financial status and should not be relied on solely.

Yield

The yield is an indicator of the return on investment of a particular security. It measures the annual income generated by the investment relative to its cost. A higher yield means a better return and vice versa. The Altman Z-score takes the yield into account as a measure of profitability.

Yield Curve

The yield curve is a graphical representation of the relationship between the yield of bonds of different maturities. It is used as a benchmark for interest rates and can provide insight into economic conditions. The Altman Z-score model takes the yield curve into account as a measure of financial risk.

Yield Management

Yield management is a pricing strategy used by companies to maximize revenue by adjusting prices based on demand. The Altman Z-score model considers yield management as a measure of profitability and takes it into account when calculating the Z-score.

Yield Spread

The yield spread is the difference between the interest rate of a high-risk security and a low-risk security. It is used as a measure of risk and can indicate changes in market sentiment. The Altman Z-score model includes the yield spread as a measure of financial risk.

Yield to Maturity

The yield to maturity is the rate of return anticipated on a bond if it is held until it matures. It includes the interest rate earned on the bond and any gain or loss in the price of the bond. The Altman Z-score model considers the yield to maturity as a measure of financial risk.

Zero-Coupon Bond

A bond that does not pay interest but instead is sold at a discount to its face value. The difference between the purchase price and the face value is the investor's return.

ZETA Analysis

Developed by Altman in the 1980s, this is a forecasting method that uses a combination of fundamental analysis, technical analysis, and regression analysis to predict the financial health of a company. ZETA stands for Zoning Evaluation Technique Analysis.

Z-Formula

Developed by Edward Altman in 1968, the Z-Score formula is used to predict the viability of a company by analyzing various financial ratios. It takes into account five key financial ratios to derive a single score that informs investors of the likelihood of bankruptcy.

Zone of Discrimination

The area between the safe and distressed zones of the Altman Z-Score model where a company's financial health is difficult to determine. It is a grey area where the Z-Score may indicate the company is in trouble but may not necessarily mean it will go bankrupt.

Zoned Industry

An industry with relatively homogeneous companies, which allows for easier identification of outliers and distinction between performers and non-performers.

Z-Score

A statistical measure that reflects the number of standard deviations by which a company's financial performance deviates from the average in its industry. In the context of Altman Z-Score, it is used to assess a company's financial health, measuring the likelihood of a company becoming bankrupt in the near future.

Z-Score Model

The Altman Z-Score model is a multivariate statistical formula designed to evaluate the financial health and strength of a company. Based on historical data, it predicts the likelihood of bankruptcy within 1-2 years for public and private companies.

Z-Statistics

A statistical tool used to calculate the probability that a company's financial position lies above or below a certain benchmark. This is especially useful when comparing a company's financial position against its peers in the industry.

Z-Table

A statistical tool that helps identify the probability of a certain Z-Score, a value obtained through the use of the Z-Formula. It is used to identify the corresponding probability of the Z-value and is typically displayed in a table format.

Z-Value

The numerical value obtained from the Z-Score formula. It helps evaluate a company's creditworthiness and indicates the likelihood of bankruptcy.